HOW MACHINES WORK

CONSTRUCTION VEHICLES

TERRY JENNINGS

W

FRANKLIN WATTS

LONDON • SYDNEY

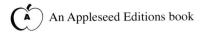 An Appleseed Editions book

First published in 2008 by Franklin Watts

Franklin Watts
338 Euston Road, London NW1 3BH

Franklin Watts Australia
Level 17/207 Kent St, Sydney, NSW 2000

© 2008 Appleseed Editions

Appleseed Editions Ltd
Well House, Friars Hill, Guestling, East Sussex TN35 4ET

Created by Q2AMedia
Series Editor: Honor Head
Book Editor: Harriet McGregor
Senior Art Director: Ashita Murgai
Designers: Harleen Mehta, Shilpi Sarkar
Picture Researchers: Amit Tigga, Poloumi Ghosh

ISBN 978 0 7496 8078 7

Dewey classification: 629.225

All words in **bold** can be found in the Glossary on pages 30–31.

Website information is correct at time of going to press. However, the publishers cannot
accept liability for any information or links found on third-party websites.

A CIP catalogue for this book is available from the British Library.

Picture credits
t=top b=bottom c=centre l=left r=right m=middle
Cover Images: © copyright AB Volvo 2008

Ljupco Smokovski/ Shutterstock: 4, Robert Harding Picture Library Ltd/ Alamy: 5tl, Jack Dagley Photography/
Shutterstock: 5tr, Semjonow Juri/ Shutterstock: 5b, Anton Gvozdikov/ Shutterstock: 6, Wally Stemberger/ Shutterstock: 7b,
John Deere: 8, Volvo: 9t, 9b, Albert H. Teich/ Shutterstock: 11t, Reino Hanninen/ Alamy: 11b, Gabe Palmer/ Alamy:12,
Bruce Burkhardt/ Flirt Collection/ Photolibrary: 13t, Anssi Ruuska/ Istockphoto: 14, Bjorn Heller/ Shutterstock: 15,
Lixxim/ Shutterstock: 17, Steven Robertson/ Istockphoto: 18, JoLin/ Shutterstock: 19, Comet, Zürich/ Nagra.ch 21b,
Robert Pernell/ Shutterstock: 22, Volvo: 23t, John Deere: 24, Volvo: 25t, 25b, Vögele America, Inc.: 26-27,
Maxim Loskuutov: 28, Dumitrescu Ciprian-Florin/ Shutterstock: 29t, Mikasa Construction Equipment: 29b

Q2AMedia Art Bank: 7t, 10, 13b, 15t, 16, 19, 20

Printed in Hong Kong

Franklin Watts is a division of Hachette Children's Books

CONTENTS

MIGHTY MACHINES

The huge machines that are used to build roads, bridges, tunnels and buildings are construction vehicles. Many of them make use of levers and pulleys.

A **lever** is a tool that allows work to be done more easily. It does this by magnifying the effort that is put into lifting, pulling, pushing or turning. The bigger the lever, the more the effort is increased. Bottle openers, wheelbarrows and crowbars are all examples of simple levers.

▶ Levers help this powerful digger scoop up heavy soil and rubble and lift it high in the air

HOW LEVERS WORK

All levers involve effort, a fulcrum and a load. The effort is the work done, such as lifting, pulling and turning. The fulcrum is the place where the lever pivots or turns. The load is the thing you want to move.

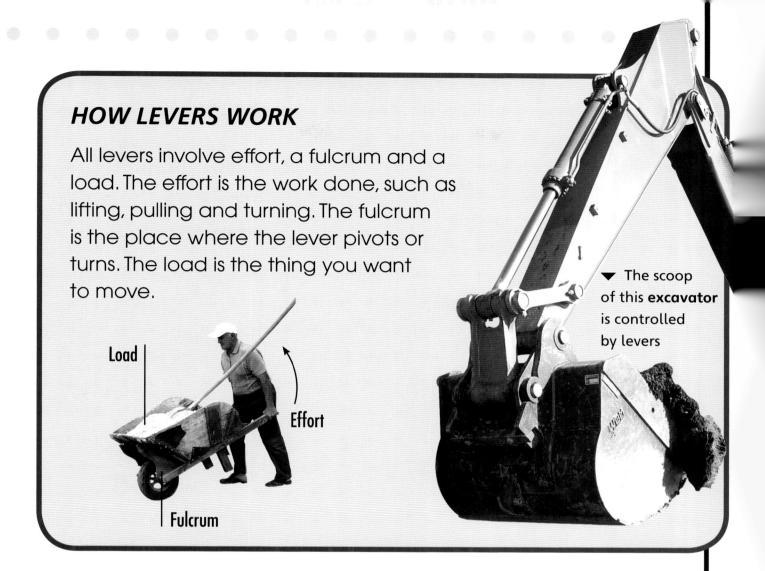

Load

Effort

Fulcrum

▼ The scoop of this **excavator** is controlled by levers

PULLEYS

Another tool used by construction machines is the **pulley** (see page 14). The more pulleys used to lift a weight, the less effort it takes.

▼ Using pulleys, this mobile crane can lift weights of up to 200 tonnes

Pulley blocks

Hook for lifting

DIGGERS AND LOADERS

Mechanical diggers need massive strength for scooping, lifting and carrying. Huge hydraulic arms give them the power they need to break up earth and rubble.

In an excavator, **hydraulic** fluid moves a **piston** up and down a **cylinder**. When fluid is pumped into the top of the cylinder, the piston moves down and the dipper arm moves up. When liquid is pumped into the bottom of the cylinder, the piston moves up and the dipper arm moves down.

Piston

Cylinder

Dipper arm

HAL

DID YOU KNOW?
In one day, the world's largest excavator can dig a hole the size of a football pitch and more than 25 m deep

HOW A HYDRAULIC RAM WORKS

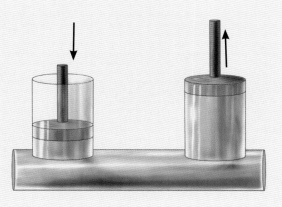

In a hydraulic system, force applied in one place is transferred to another place by squeezing a liquid. As hydraulic fluid is pumped into a cylinder, the small force at one end passes along the pipe and turns into a big force at the other end.

Hydraulic ram
Slides up and down to move the dipper arm and **bucket**

▶ Machines such as this digger use a thin hydraulic fluid that does not freeze in cold weather

Dipper arm

Joint
Acts as a fulcrum

Bucket

SCOOP, LIFT AND CARRY

A backhoe loader is a tractor, loader and backhoe all in one. The loader at the front can scoop, lift and carry. The backhoe at the rear of the machine can dig trenches and lift heavy loads. When the backhoe loader is working, hydraulic fluid pushes out **jacks** called **stabilizers**. These steady the machine and take the weight off the wheels and tyres.

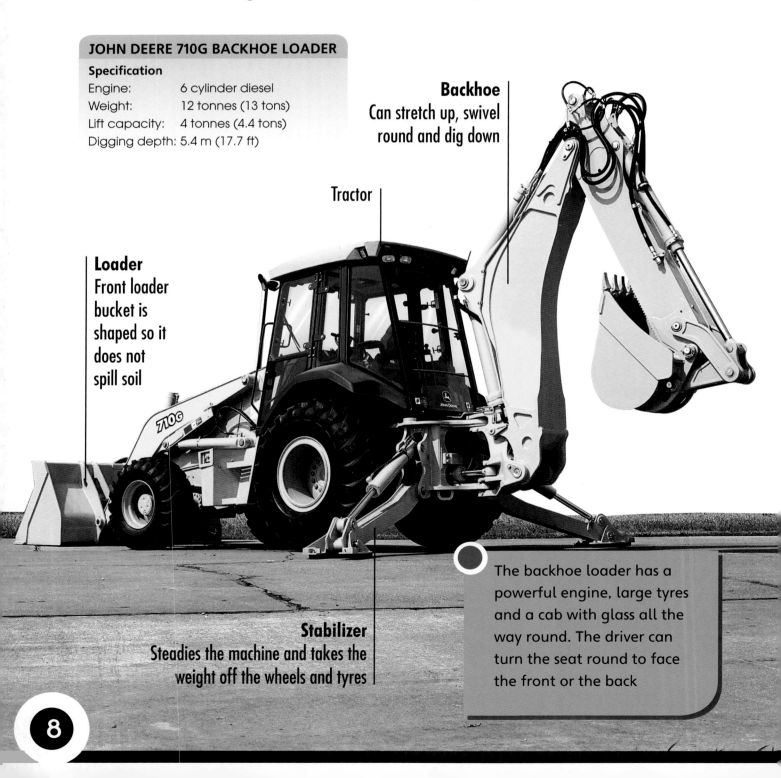

JOHN DEERE 710G BACKHOE LOADER

Specification

Engine:	6 cylinder diesel
Weight:	12 tonnes (13 tons)
Lift capacity:	4 tonnes (4.4 tons)
Digging depth:	5.4 m (17.7 ft)

Backhoe
Can stretch up, swivel round and dig down

Tractor

Loader
Front loader bucket is shaped so it does not spill soil

Stabilizer
Steadies the machine and takes the weight off the wheels and tyres

The backhoe loader has a powerful engine, large tyres and a cab with glass all the way round. The driver can turn the seat round to face the front or the back

RAMS AND JACKS

In construction machines, hydraulic systems move **rams** and jacks. A ram is a cylinder and piston which acts like the muscles of your arm. It pushes and moves parts about. Rams can be found on excavators. Jacks are also cylinders and pistons. They work like legs and feet to support and steady machines while they work.

Control for backhoe and bucket

Control for the jacks

▶ The driver needs controls to make the hydraulic systems work. These are the controls for the backhoe

MR WRIGHT

This backhoe loader is being used to dig a trench along a road, ready for large concrete drainpipes

PILEDRIVING POWER!

Imagine the force needed to hammer huge steel and concrete rods into solid ground. Powerful machines called piledrivers do this work.

A piledriver works like a giant hammer. A heavy weight is lifted high into the air. The weight is dropped again and again on to steel or concrete piles, to drive them into the ground.

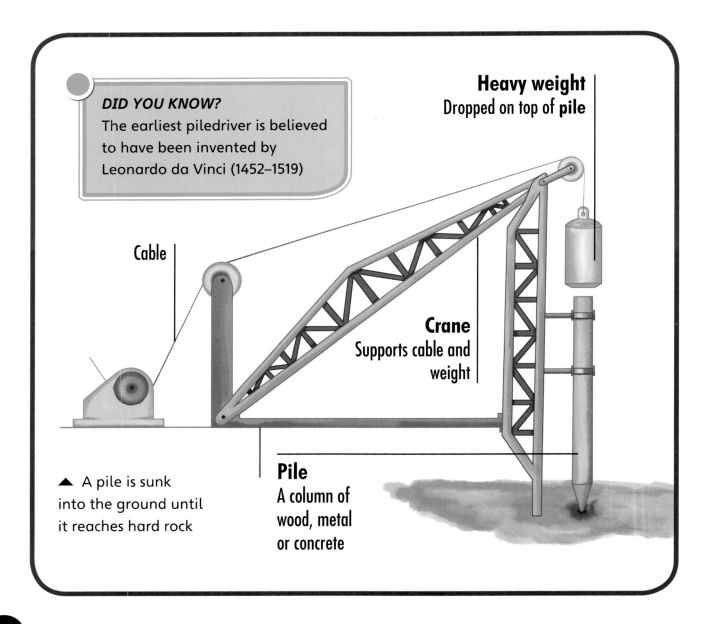

DID YOU KNOW?
The earliest piledriver is believed to have been invented by Leonardo da Vinci (1452–1519)

Cable

Heavy weight
Dropped on top of **pile**

Crane
Supports cable and weight

Pile
A column of wood, metal or concrete

▲ A pile is sunk into the ground until it reaches hard rock

WHAT IS A PILE?

A pile is a heavy shaft of steel, concrete or wood which is hammered into the ground to support a structure. Motorways, road and rail bridges, **flyovers** and **embankments** are built on piles.

◀ Workers on a construction site get ready to sink a pile into the ground

Pneumatic piledrivers use **compressed** air to raise a heavy piston inside a cylinder. The piston is dropped. The cylinder contains a mixture of fuel and air. **Friction** heats the mixture. The mixture ignites, forcing the piston back up. The cycle repeats until the machine is stopped.

Pipes
Force compressed air into cylinder

Crawler tracks
Keep vehicle from sinking into muddy ground

BLASTING

A compressor is like a pump, but instead of water, it pumps high-pressure air. Compressors can produce high-pressure air for sand blasters, which clean the outside of buildings. They can also power spray-painting machines, which produce an even coating of paint over a large wall or fence.

Sand blaster
Fires a high-pressure jet of water and sand at the wall

High above street level, a worker uses a pneumatic sand-blaster to clean the side of a tall building

DRILLING

Pneumatic drills used by construction crews work very like compressed-air piledrivers. Instead of a hammer, the drills have tough steel blades to break up earth and tarmac. The air that works the pistons in a pneumatic drill is forced into the cylinder by a compressor.

DID YOU KNOW?
A pneumatic drill can hit the road more than 1,000 times a minute

◀ Air-driven machines are safer than electrical equipment because there is no danger of getting an electric shock, even in the rain

HOW A PNEUMATIC DRILL WORKS

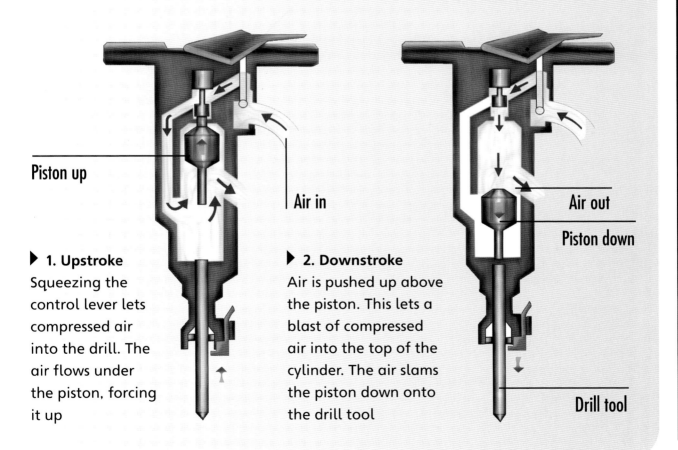

Piston up

Air in

Air out

Piston down

Drill tool

▶ **1. Upstroke**
Squeezing the control lever lets compressed air into the drill. The air flows under the piston, forcing it up

▶ **2. Downstroke**
Air is pushed up above the piston. This lets a blast of compressed air into the top of the cylinder. The air slams the piston down onto the drill tool

CRANES AND PULLEYS

Cranes use a series of simple pulleys to lift and move heavy weights, sometimes to the top of a building over 20 storeys high.

At any large construction site, you will see tall **cranes** towering above the skyline. At the base of the crane is a huge concrete block. Large bolts embedded deep in the concrete support the base and keep the crane firmly anchored to the ground.

▶ Construction crews use tower cranes to lift steel, concrete, bricks, heavy tools such as generators and many other building materials from place to place

Crane driver
Controls movement of **boom** and lifting gear

DID YOU KNOW?
The tallest tower cranes are more than 90 metres high. They are used to construct skyscrapers and other tall buildings

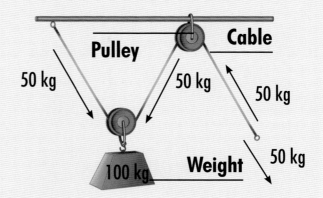

HOW A PULLEY WORKS

Pulley

Cable

50 kg

50 kg

50 kg

50 kg

100 kg

Weight

A double pulley system like this halves the effort needed to move a load, but the cable must be pulled twice as far

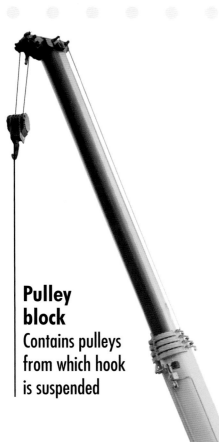

Pulley block
Contains pulleys from which hook is suspended

Boom or jib
Arm used to lift load

Hydraulic ram
Raises and lowers the boom or jib

Cab
For driving truck

◀ This mobile crane can move from place to place under its own power. The crane's hydraulic boom is like a telescope. It closes up when the crane is travelling

Outrigger
Supports and steadies crane

Cab
For operating crane

HOW A CRANE BUILDS ITSELF

How is it that a crane is able to rise as the building grows taller? The answer is that a crane builds itself! First, the base is weighted with concrete and the **jib** is assembled on the ground. Then a mobile crane lifts a 'climbing frame' onto the base. The cab and jib are put on top of the frame. The climbing frame has hydraulic rams which raise the cab up to the height of each new section.

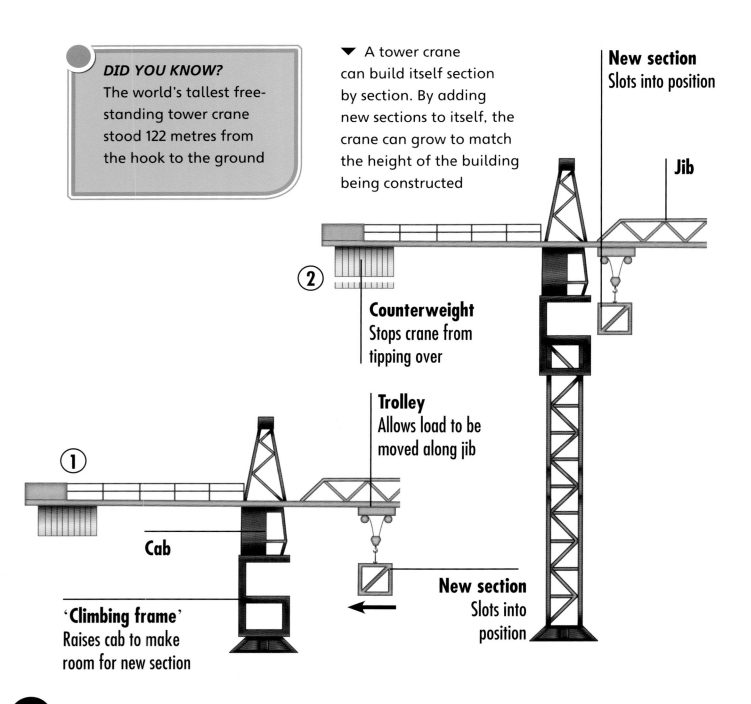

DID YOU KNOW?
The world's tallest free-standing tower crane stood 122 metres from the hook to the ground

▼ A tower crane can build itself section by section. By adding new sections to itself, the crane can grow to match the height of the building being constructed

New section
Slots into position

Jib

②

Counterweight
Stops crane from tipping over

Trolley
Allows load to be moved along jib

①

Cab

'Climbing frame'
Raises cab to make room for new section

New section
Slots into position

DRIVING A CRANE

To reach the cab, the operator either travels in a hoist (a type of lift) or climbs a ladder inside the tower. The **trolley** allows the load to be moved along the jib. It is pulled backwards and forwards by cables wound around the trolley drum. The crane's **counterweight** is made from heavy concrete blocks. It balances the weight of the jib and the load, and stops the load from pulling the crane over.

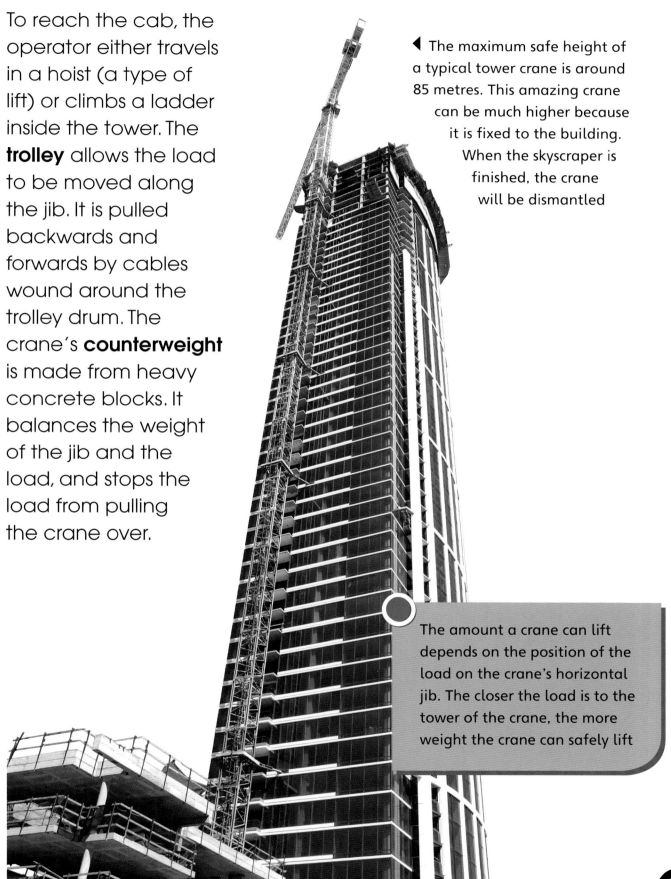

◀ The maximum safe height of a typical tower crane is around 85 metres. This amazing crane can be much higher because it is fixed to the building. When the skyscraper is finished, the crane will be dismantled

The amount a crane can lift depends on the position of the load on the crane's horizontal jib. The closer the load is to the tower of the crane, the more weight the crane can safely lift

SCREWS AND AUGERS

Did you know that screws not only fix and hold things together, they can also drill holes, carry a load, or pump up and mix materials?

AUGER DRILLS

Several construction machines use **screws** or **augers**. An auger is a screw with a wide **thread** that can be used to carry a load. A construction auger is used to drill holes for pipes or the piles for foundations. As the auger drills down, the soil spirals its way up along the thread. When the auger is full of soil, it is lifted out of the hole and cleared. It is then lowered back down to continue drilling.

▶ A construction auger being used to drill a hole. Its thread has sharp edges to cut into the ground

Rotary motor
Rotates auger as it cuts into ground

Auger
Cuts its way into ground like a corkscrew

MIXING CONCRETE

The drum of a concrete mixer truck contains a spiralling screw thread. When it turns one way, the spiralling screw thread inside mixes the concrete. When it turns the other way the screw pushes the concrete to the mouth of the drum, ready for pouring.

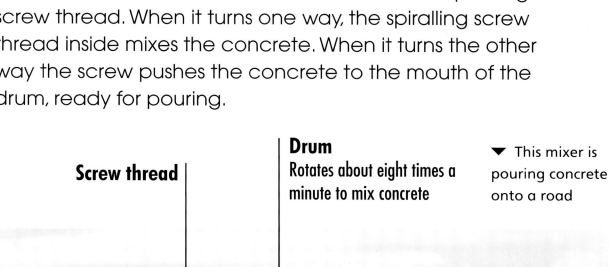

Screw thread

Drum
Rotates about eight times a minute to mix concrete

▼ This mixer is pouring concrete onto a road

Concrete
Levelled by hand

Delivery chute
Weight of concrete makes it pour down metal chute from mouth of drum

DID YOU KNOW?
The screw was one of the earliest kinds of pumps. Recent research has shown that similar machines were used in the 7th century BC

GIANT DRILLS

Tunnel-boring machines (TBMs) are like giant drills. They can cut their way underground through soil, mud and soft rocks. TBMs are used to build large tunnels to carry roads and railways through mountains, under cities, rivers and even beneath the sea. The TBM's cutting head is driven by a huge electric motor. As the head turns, its cutting rollers and teeth cut into the rock or soil ahead.

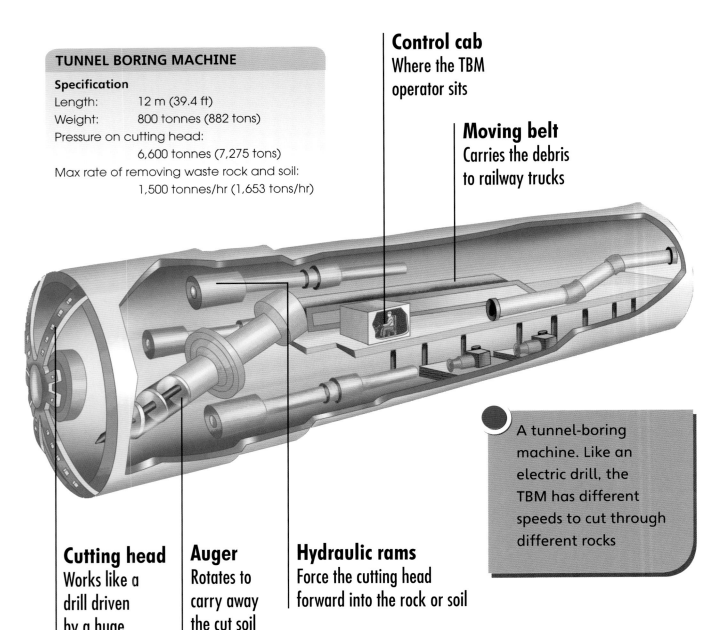

TUNNEL BORING MACHINE

Specification
Length: 12 m (39.4 ft)
Weight: 800 tonnes (882 tons)
Pressure on cutting head:
                 6,600 tonnes (7,275 tons)
Max rate of removing waste rock and soil:
                 1,500 tonnes/hr (1,653 tons/hr)

Control cab
Where the TBM operator sits

Moving belt
Carries the debris to railway trucks

A tunnel-boring machine. Like an electric drill, the TBM has different speeds to cut through different rocks

Cutting head
Works like a drill driven by a huge electric motor

Auger
Rotates to carry away the cut soil and rock

Hydraulic rams
Force the cutting head forward into the rock or soil

WASTE

A long, rotating auger scoops up and carries the soil and ground-up rock from the TBM's cutting head. This waste is lifted onto a conveyor belt. The belt carries the waste back along the TBM and dumps it in railway trucks. The railway trucks take it out of the tunnel. As the TBM bores forward, huge concrete segments are fitted in place behind it to stop the tunnel from collapsing.

DID YOU KNOW?
The world's largest tunnel-boring machine began boring a tunnel under the Yangtze River in China in 2006. This TBM has a diameter of 15.43 metres. The main cutting head alone weighs 170 tonnes

Cutting head
3.5 metres in diameter to produce a finished tunnel 2.3 metres in diameter

Electric motors
Rotate the cutting head

A tunnel-boring machine has created a new tunnel. All the TBM's systems are monitored by computers in the control cab. A laser system keeps the machine on course

PUSHING AND SHOVING

Some of the toughest construction jobs are done by machines that push and shove. They use huge engines and steel blades to clear rocks, soil and trees.

A bulldozer starts the work for a road, airport runway or railway track. Its huge metal blade can clear anything in its path. The driver can angle the bulldozer's blade to control where the soil and other materials are pushed. Bulldozers don't get stuck in mud because their weight is spread over wide **crawler tracks**.

Driver's cab
Strong steel frame protects driver if bulldozer rolls over

A large bulldozer about to start work clearing the site for a new road. The blade can be raised and lowered, and tilted forward or backward, by a pair of hydraulic rams

Blade
Made of solid steel

▼ Inside the cab
of a bulldozer

Blade control joystick
Raises, lowers and
tilts the blade

DID YOU KNOW?
The engine exhaust of a bulldozer points
upwards to avoid damage from mud
and rocks. Heavy steel prongs can be
attached to the back of the bulldozer
and used to break up hard ground

Brake pedal
Adjusts the speed of the
bulldozer and stops it

Steering wheel

SCRAPERS AND GRADERS

A grader has a cutting blade that is curved like a knife. Its job is to level the ground before a new road is laid. The grader's engine is nearly ten times as powerful as a family car and twice as powerful as a bulldozer. The grader has huge, wide tyres with deep treads to spread its weight and stop it getting stuck on muddy ground. As it moves forward, the grader's knife-like blade slices off the top layer of soil and rubble.

▶ A grader is used to clear sites of rock and soil and to shape and level rough ground ready for building roads, buildings and bridges

Driver's cab

Hydraulic ram

Huge tyres

Steel blade

GRADER

Specification

Length:	8.8 m (28.9 ft)
Height:	3.2 m (10.5 ft)
Engine:	165–185 **horsepower** diesel
Drive:	6 wheels (power drives all of the wheels, not just some of them)

HOLDING RUBBLE DILDOS

In a scraper, the soil and rubble is pushed into a container, called a bowl, by a conveyor belt of metal blades. The blades turn as the scraper moves. These metal blades, which move like the stairs of an escalator, are called the elevator. The scraper bowl can hold a load of more than 50 tonnes of rubble.

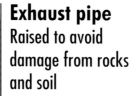

Exhaust pipe
Raised to avoid damage from rocks and soil

A grader being used to level the ground for a new road

PAVING AND ROLLING

Road paving machines are designed to lay a flat ribbon of asphalt road or airport runway. Any bumps would be a nightmare for fast traffic and aircraft.

Road paving machines move very slowly. The **hopper** is a container which is constantly filled with steaming hot **asphalt**. Steel conveyor chains carry the asphalt to the rotating blades of the auger, which spread the asphalt on the ground.

Auger

VOGELE SUPER 2100-2 ROAD PAVER

Specification

Travel speed:	up to 4.5 km/h (2.8 mph)
Hopper size:	14 tonnes (15.4 tons)
Max paving width:	13 m (42.6 ft)
Paving speed:	25 m (82 ft) per min

Screed
Flattens and smooths the asphalt

▶ A road paving machine

▶ The controls of a road paver. One set of controls drives the vehicle and another set controls laying the asphalt

Controls
For conveyor, auger and screed

Controls
For hopper and steering

IRONING THE ROAD

The road paving machine also flattens and smooths the asphalt with a heavy vibrating attachment called the screed. This works a bit like a hot iron. Electric heaters inside the screed produce heat so that it creates a smooth finish to the asphalt.

Crawler tracks
Stop the paver sinking in sticky asphalt

Hopper
Holds hot asphalt

A road paving machine being used to lay a new runway at Frankfurt Airport in Germany

RAMMERS AND ROLLERS

To make a road strong and firm, it is made of many layers. Each layer must be flattened until it is hard and smooth. Rollers and rammers use weight and **vibrations** for this work. The greatest weight comes from a large roller. The roller is driven backwards and forwards over the layers of the road, flattening and smoothing them with its heavy wheels. The front and back wheels of rollers can be steered separately.

▼ This roller weighs about as much as eight family cars. Small water sprinklers above each roller keep them clean and cool

Roller drum
Rollers vibrate as the machine moves along

Engine
Powerful 82 horsepower **diesel engine**

Water tank
Contain 365 litres of water to spray the rollers

CC222

TYPES OF ROLLER

Smaller rollers are useful for laying pavements or repairing roads. The drum vibrates as it rolls, packing the surface below to make it really solid.

A rammer machine also vibrates to flatten strips of sand, gravel or asphalt. It packs down the ground ten times harder when it is vibrating than when it is still.

DID YOU KNOW?
The wheels of some rollers are hollow so that they can be filled with water or sand to increase the weight

Engine
four-stroke petrol engine

▶ The 'foot' of this rammer vibrates as it moves along

Controls

▶ This small vibrating roller is useful for laying pavements and repairing roads

Twin drum vibrating rollers

GLOSSARY

Asphalt A sticky, tarry substance that is mixed with gravel or crushed rock to surface roads, airport runways and playgrounds

Auger A tool, rather like a large corkscrew, for boring holes in the ground or, when it rotates, for carrying loose materials

Boom The long, extending arm of a crane

Bucket The scoop of an excavator

Compressed Squeezed or pressed together

Compressor A machine that squashes or squeezes air into a smaller space

Counterweight A metal or concrete weight attached to a crane, which balances the load to stop the crane falling over

Crane A machine that is used to lift heavy objects

Crawler track A wide metal belt around a set of wheels that helps a machine to move over soft or slippery ground

Cylinder Part of an engine in which a piston moves

Diesel engine An engine that works by burning oil

Embankment A supporting ridge often made of earth or stone

Excavator A machine that digs holes

Flyover A section of a road that crosses over another route

Friction A force produced when two surfaces rub together

Hopper A container for carrying loads

Horsepower (hp) A unit for measuring the power of an engine

Hydraulic A system for operating machines that uses a liquid to push pistons and make the machine work

Lever A bar that is pushed or pulled to lift something heavy

Jack A device for lifting something heavy off the ground

Jib An arm of a crane that carries the load

Pile A heavy beam of wood, metal or concrete driven into the ground to support something

Piston A disc that moves inside a cylinder or pump

Pneumatic Filled with, or worked by, compressed air

Pulley A wheel with a groove around it to take a rope or wire, used for lifting heavy objects

Ram The piston of a hydraulic system

Screw A metal cylinder with a spiral ridge around it you

Stabilizer A device that helps to keep a machine or vehicle steady

Thread The spiral ridge on a screw

Trolley Part of a crane that runs along the jib and to which the hook is attached

Vibration Rapid to-and-fro movement

INDEX

Websites

www.kenkenkikki.jp/e_index2.html
Learn all about construction machines

www.jcbexplore.com
Games and activities for kids

http://www.pbs.org/wgbh/buildingbig/abt_chall.html
Be an engineer and make decisions about building
large structures